CUTTING-EDGE TECHNOLOGY

ALL ABOUT GREEN TECH

by Clara MacCarald

FOCUS READERS

NAVIGATOR

WWW.FOCUSREADERS.COM

Focus Readers is distributed by North Star Editions:
sales@northstareditions.com | 888-417-0195

Produced for Focus Readers by Red Line Editorial.

Content Consultant: Sailesh Adhikari, PhD, Postdoctoral Associate, Department of Sustainable Biomaterials, Virginia Polytechnic Institute and State University

Photographs ©: Shutterstock Images, cover, 1, 4–5, 7, 8–9, 11, 12–13, 15, 16, 19, 20–21, 23, 24, 26–27, 28

Library of Congress Cataloging-in-Publication Data
Names: MacCarald, Clara, 1979- author.
Title: All about green tech / Clara MacCarald.
Description: Lake Elmo, MN : Focus Readers, [2023] | Series: Cutting-edge
  technology | Includes bibliographical references and index. | Audience:
  Grades 4-6
Identifiers: LCCN 2022031719 (print) | LCCN 2022031720 (ebook) | ISBN
  9781637394717 (hardcover) | ISBN 9781637395080 (paperback) | ISBN
  9781637395783 (ebook pdf) | ISBN 9781637395455 (hosted ebook)
Subjects: LCSH: Renewable energy sources--Juvenile literature. | Recycling
  (Waste, etc.)--Juvenile literature.
Classification: LCC TJ808.2 .M326 2023 (print) | LCC TJ808.2 (ebook) |
  DDC 333.79/4--dc23/eng/20220822
LC record available at https://lccn.loc.gov/2022031719
LC ebook record available at https://lccn.loc.gov/2022031720

Printed in the United States of America
Mankato, MN
012023

ABOUT THE AUTHOR

Clara MacCarald is a freelance writer who has written more than 40 nonfiction books for kids. She lives with her daughter and a small herd of cats in an off-grid house nestled in the forests of central New York.

TABLE OF CONTENTS

CHAPTER 1

A Sunny Hike 5

CHAPTER 2

Why Green Tech? 9

CHAPTER 3

Types of Green Tech 13

HOW IT WORKS

Solar Panels 18

CHAPTER 4

Challenges of Green Tech 21

CHAPTER 5

The Future of Green Tech 27

Focus on Green Tech • 30
Glossary • 31
To Learn More • 32
Index • 32

A SUNNY HIKE

You and your mom are on a camping trip. It's a bright, sunny day. You plan to hike to a waterfall. You can't wait to take pictures. But when you pick up your phone, the battery is dead.

Fortunately, your mom is prepared. She pulls a device from her bag. It unfolds. Inside are small solar panels.

Hikers can use small, portable solar panels to get power on the go.

These panels can use sunlight to make electricity. Your mom plugs your phone into the device. Then she straps the panels to her backpack.

As you hike, the sun shines on the panels. They soak up energy from the light. They turn this energy into electricity. By the time you reach the waterfall, your phone is charged. You unplug it and start taking pictures. Thanks to green tech, you can capture the beautiful view.

Solar panels are just one example of green tech. Green tech is **technology** that reduces the harmful effects of human activity on the environment. One of the

Producing power from wind or sunlight is less damaging to the environment than burning fuel.

biggest ways humans pollute the planet is through energy production. So, many types of green tech provide cleaner ways to make power. Other green tech saves **resources** or reduces waste.

CHAPTER 2

WHY GREEN TECH?

Many human activities are bad for the environment. For example, people burn **fossil fuels** to get energy. Burning these fuels releases greenhouse gases into Earth's atmosphere. These gases trap heat. Earth needs some greenhouse gases to stay warm enough to support living things. However, people have sent

Power plants that burn fossil fuels, such as coal, pollute the air.

too much of these gases into the air. The added gases are causing **climate change**.

This crisis is causing serious problems. Higher temperatures are melting ice sheets. Sea levels are rising. Areas along the coasts are more likely to flood. Deadly weather events are increasing, too. These include heat waves, wildfires, and storms.

Unless people stop relying on fossil fuels, these problems will continue to get worse. Green tech can help people produce power from other sources. These sources don't add greenhouse gases to the air.

Trash is another huge problem. Garbage dumps can release harmful

Trash from electronic devices can be dangerous. It often contains poisonous chemicals.

chemicals into land, air, or water. Trash can also end up in the ocean. There, it breaks down into tiny pieces. The pieces can hurt animals or make them sick. Some green tech helps cut down on trash by recycling. Other tech can reduce the resources people use in the first place.

CHAPTER 3

TYPES OF GREEN TECH

Some types of green tech focus on renewable energy. This energy comes from sources that will not run out. Examples include sunlight, wind, and water. Solar tech captures energy from the sun. This power can be used to heat water for people's homes. Or the energy can be turned into electricity.

Unlike fossil fuels, renewable resources such as sunlight will not run out.

Turbines help people get power from wind or water. These machines use turning blades to produce power. A wind turbine looks like a tall tower. Its long blades spin when the wind blows. The motion of the blades powers a **generator**.

Hydroelectricity uses the motion of water. A dam blocks a stream or a river. Water builds up behind the dam. Pipes or tunnels allow the water to fall to a lower height. The falling water spins a turbine.

Renewable energy can also come from the planet itself. Some green tech uses heat from below Earth's surface. Other forms of energy come from **organic matter**, such as food waste or plants.

Dams use running water to produce electric power.

People use this matter to produce fuel, heat, or electricity.

Gasoline-powered vehicles are a major source of air pollution. So, green tech helps find new ways to power vehicles. Electric cars are one example. These cars use power stored in batteries. Instead

 Factories sort, wash, shred, and reshape plastic so it can be used again.

of burning gasoline, electric cars can be recharged. Moreover, they don't release greenhouse gases when they run.

Green tech can reduce waste, too. It can improve **manufacturing**. For example, designers are making products that last longer and create less waste. They are using less-**toxic** materials. And they make products and packaging easier to recycle. People can melt or take apart certain items to make new products. Green tech can even make plastic from plant fiber. This type of plastic breaks down more easily than regular plastic.

PLASTIC ROADS

Some roadways are made with recycled plastic. Workers tear up plastic waste and melt it. Then they mix it with stones, sand, tar, and other materials. Next, they spread this mixture on the ground. Paving with plastic helps keep waste out of landfills. However, melting the plastic can give off greenhouse gases. Experts are also concerned the roads could break down and pollute the environment.

SOLAR PANELS

Solar panels turn the sun's energy into electricity. The panels are made up of many tiny solar cells. These cells contain a material that can conduct electricity when sunlight hits them. A layer of glass or clear plastic goes over the cells. The covering protects the cells. But it lets light pass through.

When sunlight hits a cell, the cell takes in some of the light's energy. This energy causes **electrons** to start flowing. The flowing electrons create an electric current. Metal lines on the panel carry this current away from each cell. They guide the current to an inverter. The inverter changes this current into a type of electricity that can be used in people's homes.

People can set up solar panels on the ground or roofs. Large groups of panels are called solar

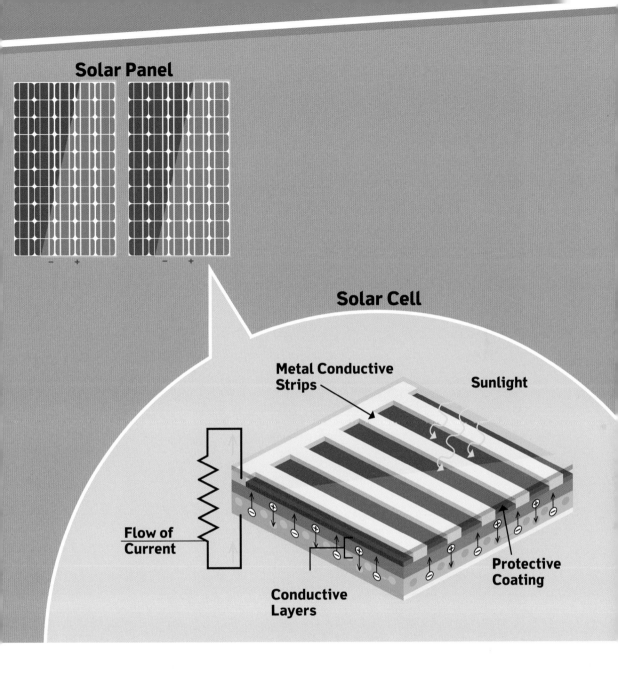

Solar Panel

Solar Cell

Metal Conductive Strips

Sunlight

Flow of Current

Conductive Layers

Protective Coating

farms. Solar farms generate enough electricity to power many homes. They may include thousands of panels.

CHAPTER 4

CHALLENGES OF GREEN TECH

Green tech isn't perfect. It still uses up natural resources. In some cases, people dig deep mines to get them. Mines can harm the environment.

Making green tech also requires energy. Some of that energy comes from fossil fuels. And when green tech gets old, it can create toxic waste.

Solar panels may contain harmful chemicals, but old and broken panels get thrown away.

Some green tech can harm wildlife. Dams require flooding large areas of land. They may block animals' paths through streams and rivers. Solar farms can also disrupt animal habitats. And birds can die as a result of hitting spinning wind turbines.

SAFER SOLUTIONS

To protect birds, people avoid building wind farms where birds often nest or fly. Some farms have ways to detect birds, too. For example, most wild condors wear radio trackers. Antenna towers near wind farms can check for their signals. If a condor is nearby, the farm can stop the turbines from spinning. Another system uses a computer program to scan the sky for approaching eagles.

Wind turbines need open areas with steady wind in order to work well.

It can also be challenging to get renewable energy where and when people need it. Wind and solar power are not constant. The sun goes down at night or gets covered by clouds. Wind can blow hard or not at all. Storing large amounts of power can be difficult and expensive.

Power is a problem for electric cars, too. These cars need places to charge

Scientists are working on solar-powered charging stations for electric cars.

their batteries. In many areas, there are few charging stations. And charging a car takes much longer than adding gasoline to a tank. Plus, most electricity still comes from burning fossil fuels. Using it contributes to climate change.

Recycling has limits as well. After several rounds of recycling, paper becomes too weak to reuse. Most plastic can be recycled just once or twice. And some types of plastic cannot be recycled at all.

Cost is another challenge. Renewable energy must compete with other energy sources. Even if it can save people money in the long run, making the switch can be very expensive. For example, electric cars help people save on gasoline. But these cars cost too much for some people to buy. Recycling can also be expensive. After communities gather waste for recycling, they must pay companies to process it. Those companies can charge high prices.

CHAPTER 5

THE FUTURE OF GREEN TECH

In 2021, only 11.4 percent of energy around the world came from green energy sources. World leaders made plans to use more green tech. And scientists continued to improve it.

Some scientists studied ways to recycle more types of plastic. Others explored new technology. Floating wind

Placing solar panels in parking lots can help cities use more renewable energy.

Scotland is one of several countries that has begun building wind farms in the ocean.

turbines are one example. These turbines can anchor in deep water offshore. Winds there are stronger than winds close to land. Scientists also helped solar tech produce more power at lower costs.

In 2022, solar was the cheapest source of renewable energy. Its use was also increasing the fastest. Improved batteries could more easily store solar energy. In many cases, solar and wind energy were cheaper than fossil fuels.

A few countries have aimed to make electricity only from clean sources in the future. Solar and wind will be a big part of meeting that goal.

HYDROGEN CARS

People can use hydrogen gas to produce power. Some cars use hydrogen as fuel. These cars give off water rather than greenhouse gases. So far, high costs have kept people from buying hydrogen cars. And there are not many places cars can get hydrogen. However, scientists continue working on solutions. They hope to make hydrogen fuel cheaper and easier to buy.

FOCUS ON
GREEN TECH

Write your answers on a separate piece of paper.

1. Write a paragraph describing the main ideas of Chapter 2.

2. Which form of green tech do you think is most promising? Why?

3. Which of these inventions can help provide people with renewable energy?

   A. solar panels
   B. plant-based plastic
   C. gasoline-powered cars

4. Which type of green tech turns the energy of motion into electricity?

   A. wind turbines
   B. hydrogen fuel
   C. organic matter

Answer key on page 32.

GLOSSARY

climate change
A human-caused global crisis involving long-term changes in Earth's temperature and weather patterns.

electrons
Charged particles that can be in atoms or on their own.

fossil fuels
Energy sources that come from the remains of plants and animals that died long ago.

generator
A machine that turns the energy of motion into electricity.

manufacturing
The process of making items that will be sold.

organic matter
Material that comes from a living thing, such as a plant or animal.

resources
Things of value.

technology
Machines and devices created using science.

toxic
Harmful or poisonous.

TO LEARN MORE

BOOKS

Cooke, Joanna K. *Energy from Wind*. Lake Elmo, MN: Focus Readers, 2022.

Kehoe, Rachel. *Future Fuels to Fight Climate Change*. Lake Elmo, MN: Focus Readers, 2023.

Kenney, Karen Latchana. *Solar Energy*. North Mankato, MN: Capstone Press, 2019.

NOTE TO EDUCATORS

Visit **www.focusreaders.com** to find lesson plans, activities, links, and other resources related to this title.

INDEX

battery, 5, 15, 24, 28

climate change, 10, 24

electric cars, 15–16, 23, 25
electrons, 18
environment, 6, 9, 17, 21

fossil fuels, 9–10, 21, 24, 29

generator, 14
greenhouse gases, 9–10, 16–17, 29

hydroelectricity, 14
hydrogen cars, 29

mines, 21

plastic, 17–18, 25, 27
pollution, 7, 15, 17

recycling, 11, 24–25, 27

renewable energy, 13–14, 23, 25, 28
resources, 7, 21

solar panels, 5–6, 18–19

trash, 10–11

waste, 7, 14, 16–17, 21, 25
wind turbines, 14, 22

Answer Key: 1. Answers will vary; **2.** Answers will vary; **3.** A; **4.** A